Feathers

50 Things You Can Do in 50 Seconds or Less to Lighten Up and Set Yourself Free

Robin L. Silverman

D1509616

ISBN: 1533395454
ISBN-13: 9781533395450
Library of Congress Control Number: 2016909411
CreateSpace Independent Publishing Platform
North Charleston, South Carolina

Dedication

*To Archie and Charlie. You are the feathers
that tickle my heart.*

Contents

THERE IS NO table of contents in this book because it is meant to be used as an intuitive tool that connects you to gentle suggestions that your thinking mind would likely reject when you are in a negative state.   You have probably heard Albert Einstein's famous quote, "you cannot solve a problem with the same mind that created it." So instead of trying to figure out what would work, let yourself be guided. See "How to use this book" for more information.

Acknowledgments

THIS BOOK WOULD not have been possible without the instruction and guideposts provided by numerous authors and teachers whose goal, like mine, is to expand and enhance wellbeing and happiness on our planet. I am deeply grateful for the knowledge, inspiration and love for humanity they have shared with me and countless others.

Introduction

I'VE ALWAYS LOVED people, and have met a lot of wonderful ones in my life. Many of them were doing everything "right"—they were/are kind, loving, generous, intelligent, hard-working, decent people. But for too many, things kept going wrong for them, or happiness seemed to elude them. Even my own positive outlook on life kept getting marred by experiences that seemed to pull me back or down.

I wanted to break free. So I started searching for answers.

Hundreds of books, dozens of seminars and thousands of days of experimenting later, I learned what so many have come to know: that everything, including us, is energy in various forms, and that these forms exist in an infinite field of energy from which they originate and return. All this energy cannot be created or destroyed; only transformed.

Who and what does the transforming? Most of the time, we do, but we don't realize we're doing it. The science of physics explains how the act of observation changes what is being observed. Unfortunately, too much of the time, we're paying attention to what bothers, frustrates, angers or upsets us, so we unwittingly are creating more of what we don't want, rather than accelerating the arrival of what we do.

There are three good reasons for this. First, we are biologically designed to survive. Long ago, we ran away from sabre tooth tigers. But over time, we have evolved into a species of world-class worriers. Each of us, every day, is bombarded with somewhere between 50,000 and 80,000 thoughts in our own brains (never mind the negative news, attitudes and problems that surround us), and 80% of these are negative. This supposedly protects us from potential pain and destruction and helps us survive. "I **don't** want to be late!" "There **isn't** going to be time!" "I **can't** save that much money." "I **never** win." We repeat these negative thoughts over and over, over and over. In fact, 90% of what we think is simply a rehash of what we thought yesterday. Brain scientists tell us that the consequence of this is that eventually, our brains become hard-wired to the negative. The saying is: "neurons that fire together, wire together." In other words, in trying to survive, we become wired to fear, frustration, disappointment and discontent, and tend to focus on it incessantly.

The second reason for this flood of negativity is that we tend to socialize around the negative. You often hear people say, "I feel your pain," but you almost never hear anyone say, "I share your happiness." If a friend asks you how you are and you reply, "Great! I just won the lottery; we're taking a trip around the world and my lover is sending me roses every Monday," don't be surprised if your friend says, "Well, that's nice," and walks away. (And if you throw in that you just lost ten pounds, that conversation is truly over!) If you want to have friends, there has to be a "but" in there somewhere, as in "I just won the lottery, but the taxes are a killer," or "We're taking a trip around the world, but we're wiping out our savings to do it" or "My lover is sending me roses every Monday, but he missed my birthday two years in a row." In other words, if you want to have friends, you'd better have something to be publicly unhappy about.

The third reason why we tend to focus on the negative is because we need to have something to do. If nothing went wrong, we wouldn't be able to put it right. This is where jobs come from. Every product or service fixes a problem or serves a purpose, or it wouldn't exist.

All this negative thinking not only affects our attitudes and motivation; it also has another unwelcome consequence. Every thought generates an emotion. We think; we feel. Some people pull the word apart and talk about e-motion, referring to energy in motion. That motion can be fast or slow, dark or light, depending on the emotion being experienced at that moment.

Our bodies can't tell the difference between a negative thought and an actual bad experience. So every time we worry, it's as if that bad, frightening or unwanted situation is actually occurring, which causes the molecules and atoms in our cells to vibrate in uncomfortable and unnatural ways. This not only feels bad; it can potentially make us sick. Vibrational malaise is sometimes called "dis-ease." Far too many of us bash our bodies with the powerful one-two punch of negative thought and emotion all day and night, which can be mentally and emotionally exhausting.

If we were just harming ourselves, that would be one thing, but all this negative energy affects the people around us because we have multiple energy bodies, not just the physical ones we can see with our naked eyes. Some people are able to see auras, and some of the energy radiating from us can be seen on Kirlian photographs. Skilled Reiki practitioners and acupuncturists, among others who apply energy methodologies in their work, are also able to detect and move energy. It's not just our attitudes people can detect; it's the nature of our entire vibrational fields, which have no solid boundaries. This is why we can feel some people coming down the hall, long before we can see them. We all know people who give off "bad vibes" with their unhappiness. We hate being around them, and often feel tired or physically pained if we are forced to spend time in their company. So we're not only hurting ourselves; we are potentially hurting others.

There's another problem, too. As author Mike Dooley points out, thoughts can become things. As any quantum physicist will tell you, subatomic particles respond to human observation. In other words, your attention on any one thing is enough to create a play of particles and waves that are the foundation of matter, and what you focus on is yours. Unfortunately, since our negative thoughts produce negative emotions, most of us are putting out a whole lot of negative energy that gives us more of what we don't want than what we do. Haven't you noticed that when you pay attention to your problems, you just get bigger problems, not the solutions you crave? This is why, on the mornings you think you have gotten up on the wrong side of the bed, your car won't start, you're overdrawn at the bank and the most annoying person in the office sticks like glue to your desk.

Finally, there's also the impact that all this density has on our intuition. Just when we need solutions the most, we block them. We can't hear the voice of our heart when our head is screaming, and we are blinded to helpful signs and signals around us when our attention is on what is or could potentially be wrong. The answer we need could be right in front of us, but we won't see it.

The irony is that all of this is just a game. Although most of us take life very seriously, those who have had experiences of bliss and oneness point out that true, lasting peace lies within us; the very core of our nature. Peace is not something that we have to seek, and it isn't temporary; it's something we all have, and can reveal.

As odd as it may seem, the key is not getting rid of negative thinking. As anyone who has tried to have relentlessly positive thinking can tell you, it's exhausting. It's like trying to hold up a falling ceiling. In addition, if you got rid of your negative thinking, you'd likely be living without your survival instinct, your friends or your job. But there are ways to unplug from the negative just long enough to reconnect to the energies of happiness and peace that lie within you and allow their positive potential to be broadcast into all aspects of your life.

While meditation is probably the ideal way to shift out of negative thinking and reconnect with higher energy states, not everyone has the time or patience to do it, particularly during busy work days or evenings when the demands of family, friends or more work continue to run high. The fastest, easiest way to feel better mentally and physically while simultaneously raising your vibrational state is to unplug from the negative temporarily. Not forever—remember that the negative is useful, providing the contrast we need to continue to make choices and create. But simple shifts like these can help you feel better fast. Picking up one of the feathers in this book can provide instant mental and physical relief while energetically opening the door to some fun surprises as you lift the dense energy fog in and around you and let in—and out--some light.

These ideas are very simple, but they work for many people. You don't need to know anything about energy sciences to do them. Practice them often, and you'll find you have more vibrancy and enjoy better outcomes in your life than you ever thought possible. Don't let their simplicity fool you: they can be powerful tools to reveal the happiness that has been hiding inside you all along while they connect you to more of what you want. As you've already discovered, struggle and frustration are not the paths to joy. Pick up a feather, lighten up, and set yourself free from the density that has been blocking the beauty and peace that *is* you, and is yours.

Wishing you joy!

Robin L. Silverman

How to use this book.

WHILE YOU CAN certainly read through this book from start to finish if you want to, the best way to use it is to open it at random whenever you're feeling stressed, frustrated, disappointed, angry or unhappy. Doing so will likely give you a suggestion that will help you get unblocked and get your energy flowing again. This is why there is no table of contents in this book; you don't want your negative thinking mind to make the choice for you. By taking the random approach, you override what you think you should do to connect with what you could possibly do, which is more likely to give you the relief needed to balance the negative energy you're feeling at that moment. This is especially true if you state your conscious intention before you do it.

Ideally, say aloud, "Connect me to what will help me now." Or, "Connect me to happiness." Then open the book.

Stating your intention aloud performs multiple functions: 1) it gets you out of your all those annoying voices in your head and into the safety of the moment; 2) it releases sound vibrations with a tone and character that will connect you to what best matches your state of being at the moment (assuming you're holding the physical book; I'll make a suggestion about reading it on devices in a moment); 3) it reminds you of your intention, which helps you focus on feeling better.

If you're reading the book on a device, simply amend the statement slightly: "Connect me to the Feather number that will help me now." Then pause. Close your eyes. Each of us is "audient" in some way—clairvoyant, clairaudient, clairsentient—so you're likely to get a visual image in your imagination; "hear" a number; or start scrolling through the pages with your eyes still closed until you get a physical sense that you should stop. You can also use these same approaches with the physical book.

If you're in a setting where you'd prefer not to speak aloud or close your eyes, just open the book to the first page that catches your attention. The method you use is less important than simply giving yourself permission to feel better, accepting what might make that possible right now, and taking action.

Are feathers scientific, or are they just fun stuff?

The answer is that they are both. Each feather is based on principles that can be found in physics, noetic science, or energetics. Physics is the study of energy in a state of transformation; noetic science research focuses on the application of consciousness to matter and experience; and energetics is the study of the human biofield. Together, these three sciences provide the foundation for all Fullistic® approaches, which combine your inner self with your higher self in this moment. The combination of the three sciences aligns what is in you and around you with what is coming through you. Fullistics creates flow in multiple dimensions, which opens the door to delight. You can read more about Fullistics on my website: www.fullistic.com.

While I am not a scientist or researcher, I have studied the work of those who are for more than three decades, and have both spoken about these approaches in keynote speeches and taught them in workshops. I also regularly use them myself. I am an avid collector of true stories of when people enjoy breakthrough experiences, which can result when a shift of perspective reveals what seemed to be hidden in plain sight.

And yes, feathers are meant to be fun. I believe in approaching life with a combination of down-to-earth practicality and light-hearted spirit in most situations. My hope is that you will find this book to be an enjoyable, useful tool that helps increase both your pleasure and personal peace.

What results can I expect?

The feathers in this book will help release you from whatever dense, heavy energy is making you feel unhappy in the moment. It's a temporary fix, not a permanent one. These are tips and hints, not pronouncements or prescriptions. They're meant to be fast, easy and fun—just enough to help you lighten up a little so you can get more satisfaction and pleasure from each day.

When you try one of these feathers, the state of your energy bodies shifts slightly, and you'll likely feel a little lighter, freer, happier. When that happens, you may experience a shift for the better in your circumstances, since you just raised the vibration of your energy bodies. Remember: like attracts like. In addition, you'll likely discover that there truly is a core of happiness and peace inside you, and when you let it out, things can change for the better not only for you, but those whose lives touch yours.

Note, however, that it's easy to fall back into denser energy states, since so many of our thoughts are negative and we are biologically designed to constantly scan our environment for potential causes of pain so we can protect ourselves. Go easy on yourself when this happens. Just pick up another feather when you can.

Remember, too, that this is not a book about positive thinking. It's about releasing dense energy, which reveals better things in you and the world around you. It's like seeing the fog roll out and noticing the sun has been shining all along. As said earlier, trying to think positively all the time can be exhausting. However, allowing the natural positive state of your being to shine through without blocking it feels great.

Note if you are continually feeling sad, depressed, angry, unhappy, guilty, ashamed or any other negative state of mind, this book is not likely to help much, if at all. Please seek professional care. There are many wonderful doctors, therapists and professionals who are skilled and ready to help you. This book can be a lovely addition to professional care; share it with your doctor or therapist, who might guide you in new ways to use it in your treatment.

Expect that things can get better and better, once you make the choice that they can be.

Why are there only 50 Feathers?

There are only 50 ideas in this little book because having that number matches the 50 second title. I suspect there are millions and millions of feathers that help people lighten up, and would love to have you share what works for you, whether or not your chosen approach takes 50 seconds or less. Join the Fullistic® Living Facebook family to post your own feathers and read what others have to say as well.

The 50 Feathers

1
Ride the tide

THE FASTEST WAY to feel happy is to stop fighting the tide of unhappiness that may be surrounding
you now. It's easy to do that: just go with the flow
of the negative energy. Decide: I **don't** want to feel
this way! Or, I **can't** live like this a moment longer!
Author Eckhart Tolle, in his book, "*The Power of Now,*"
describes an experience where he felt overwhelmed
by the negative voice in his head. Suddenly, he heard
a voice say, "Resist nothing," and he fell into a state of
bliss. Diving into the negative is not necessarily going
to lead to an enlightenment experience, but accepting and flowing with it removes the vibrational density
caused by resistance.

If you really can't stand allowing the negative, try
doing a 180-degree flip on it, transforming a clear
negative into a clear positive. For example: "I don't

want to feel this way!" could become "I **do** want to feel happy and peaceful!" Or, "I can't live like this a moment longer!" could become, "I'm ready **now** to start living happily!" In fact, the clearer you are about what you don't want, the easier it becomes to focus on what you really, truly **do** want. This will quickly snap you out of the negative and into the positive, but beware: trying to be ultra-positive when you're feeling pulled to the dark side can be exhausting, and it's easy to slip back.

Another approach is to see if you can create an incoming and outflowing tide of positivity and negativity using a little visualization. Imagine a beautiful sunny day on your favorite beach, with sunbeams dancing on the water. Place yourself in the water to your comfort level: either standing on the shore, with the cool tide licking your feet or in the water up to your knees, hips, waist or shoulders. The idea is to feel the pull of the tide as it moves in and out. Close your eyes, and feel the cool, sparkling water bring you joy and peace. When it pulls away, imagine it taking all your stress and tension with you.

Whatever tidal approach you select, stay with it until you feel the shift you want. You'll know when you've done it because your body will tell you. Your heart will stop pounding, your stomach won't feel as though someone put a vice around it and you'll feel like you can breathe again.

If you're still fighting the flow, stop. Unplug from these thoughts and this situation completely, and distract yourself. Take 50 seconds and find your tide. It's a fast, easy way to get in the flow again.

2
Watch yourself

WE ARE ALWAYS observing others, but almost never watch ourselves in action. It is easy for us to pass judgment on how other people act when they feel stressed. "If only you would stand up for yourself," we say, or, "why don't you..." We are always clear about what others should do, because our fight-or-flee instincts think it's their problem, not ours. When it comes to getting ourselves out of a blue funk, it's best to look at yourself, rather than others.

The next time you feel stressed, take 50 seconds and turn your well-developed skills of observation on yourself. Mentally stand back and take a good, hard look. Hear the angry or sullen tone in your voice. Notice your posture, which is probably hunched over or twisted up in pretzel-like knots. Pay attention to what you are doing. Are your actions contributing to

8
Let go

GET PHYSICAL WITH your stress. Try Progressive Muscle Relaxation, where you start at one end of your body and work your way to the other, deliberately tightening and then releasing each muscle group along the way.

Start at the top of your body. Tighten the muscles in your face; hold for a second, and then let go. Squeeze your shoulders up towards your ears, and then let go. Bend your arms at the elbows, squeeze, and let go. Close your hands into fists; let go.

Continue working your way down your body, all the way to your ankles and feet, tightening each muscle group as much as you can, and then fully letting go. Although ideally, Progressive Muscle Relaxation is done in 15 minutes, 50 seconds is enough to release some accumulated tension, fast. You can find many videos and books on Progressive Muscle Relaxation if you want to learn the technique fully.

Another way to let go physically is to shake it off. Stand up. Let your hands drop to your sides. Shake your hands, letting your wrists go floppy. Slowly raise your arms, until your hands are over your head, continuing the floppy/shaking motion along the way. Once your arms are over your head, get the rest of your body into the action. Shake your torso. Shake out your legs. Shake and shimmy until you feel free. (If you have any physical conditions that would make this challenging, ask your physician for modifications to this approach.)

When you're having trouble getting your mind under control, switch your attention to your body instead. Letting go liberates trapped energy. It wakes you up and helps you feel better fast.

9
Look inside

THE FASTEST, EASIEST way out of a dense energy state is to tune inward to recognize the glorious, vibrant energy being you are.

It's simple to do. Put your attention on your hands. Notice their physical appearance, but then let your imagination take you inside. "See" the bones, the blood, the nerves and tissues.

Then let the powerful combination of your imagination and your sixth sense take you to a subatomic level. Sense the molecules dancing. See the atoms at play.

Finally, go one level more, until all you see or sense is light. As any physicist will tell you, atoms are mostly empty space, light in motion.

If your 50 seconds isn't up yet, let your awareness expand to your entire body. Relax into the radiance and peace of your own light.

Now...where did that darkness go?

10
Look for something that's <u>NOT</u> wrong

MOST OF THE time, our thoughts are focused on what is bothering or annoying us. We tend to ignore the things that are not bothering us because, well— they're not bothering us! That's a mistake, because when we focus on what's **not** wrong, we feel safer. The safer and more comfortable we feel, the less defensive our thoughts become. And the less defensive our thoughts, the more likely we are to be open to and have experiences that make us feel happy and free.

Right now, this instant, scan the area immediately around you. If you are in a place you do not like, go within and scan your body, both inside and out. Let something that is *not* wrong impress you. Is the room _not_ smoke-filled? Is your chair _not_ rickety? Which parts of your body are _not_ aching or _don't_ look bad?

You do not have to search for a long list of things that are _not_ wrong in order to get the benefits of this. Finding just one thing will help. Concentrate on knowing more about that one thing. If it's the _un_-smoky air, breathe it in fully and completely. See what that feels like, sounds like...maybe even how it tastes. If it's the fact that you _don't_ have a headache, get a sense of the blood flowing freely, nourishing every cell, synapse and neuron. Choose whatever appeals to you most, and savor your mental oasis. The more playfully you can do this, the better.

Do this often, and you will soon discover that there is more that is right than wrong in your life. At the very least, you'll strike more of a balance. Fifty seconds later, you'll feel much, much better.

11
Look for something that's going <u>right</u>

ONCE YOU MASTER the game of finding what's not wrong, try looking for something around you that you feel is **right.**

Yes, there's a difference. When you focus on what's right, you feel blessed. Abundant. You are no longer looking for safety; you are creating balance in what otherwise might feel like a life lacking in simple pleasures. In a basic way, you're beginning to acknowledge the feeling of "all is right in my world."

So take 50 seconds and look. You might think the light in the room is just right. Or the sound of a child laughing. Or someone smiling, offering another person a cup of coffee. It could be the way your clothes feel against your skin, or the memory of your favorite song that simply pops into your head as soon as you choose to do this. You might find rightness in the flavor of a stick of gum or the way lettuce crunches in your sandwich as you take a bite. If you need a boost of ideas, read Barbra Ann Kipfer's book, ***14,000 Things to Be Happy About***. It's a 600-page list of things that are right. Better still, start your own list, and add to it every day.

As before, welcome the sensations of what you've chosen. Experience them with all five of your senses. Allow the pleasure of them to pour through your body. Feel the vice grip of your thoughts letting go. And watch your spirit come out to play.

You can play this game anywhere, any time. Try it on your morning commute: notice how most drivers are driving safely. Try it in the office: most people are doing exactly the right thing they're supposed to be doing. Try it in the grocery store as you fill your cart with things you enjoy eating.

Isn't it a relief to see how well life can work?

12
Change the scenery

ONE OF THE simplest ways to release the vibrational impact of your current location is to leave it for 50 seconds. Get up from your desk and walk down the hall. If you can't leave your desk, turn your chair around and face a different direction.

If neither of these ideas works, let your imagination take you wherever you'd like to go. Close your eyes and imagine your favorite spot. Pretend that you are actually there right now, and describe it out loud. Tell what you see, hear, smell, feel and taste in vivid detail. For instance, don't just say something is "pretty." Bring it to life: "The Caribbean sea is as deep and blue as a rare sapphire. It's so clean and clear that I can see to the bottom of the water. The fish are brilliantly colored, with yellow scales that gleam like an August sun, reds that look like ripe cherries and purple the color of a royal velvet robe." If you can, record what you are saying, so you can play it back the next time you are feeling stressed.

If you're in a situation where you can't close your eyes, speak aloud or record anything, then just stop talking and let your mind wander. People do it all the time. If someone calls you out or insists on your attention, just admit that you weren't listening closely and ask them to repeat what they said. Most people will be happy to do so.

If you need help, listen to 50 seconds of any well-phrased passage from an audiobook. Or purchase some guided imagery that will walk and talk you through a place of beauty. There are numerous channels and videos available now that are both visual and aural journeys through relaxing locations.

Change the scenery, and you'll find that you'll have new energy to get on with the rest of your life.

13
Throw it out

ONE OF THE greatest sources of dense energy and stress is clutter. Old papers and magazines, unused gifts, clothes that are out of fashion or that don't fit, lamps or furniture you don't use, outgrown toys, anything unrepaired—it's all basically stagnant energy that keeps you trapped. The argument of "it has sentimental value" keeps you mired in the past. And the thought, "we might need it someday" only adds to the awareness that you believe that trouble could overtake you at any time. Whether it does or it doesn't, I've never seen an example where a lot of old junk was the solution to a crisis.

At work, clutter looks like a ridiculously full email inbox; unread texts; a calendar full of back-to-back meetings, piles of paper and the remnants of yesterday's lunch in an unwashed insulated bag that you forgot to take home. It's all just energy that's keeping you trapped.

Being surrounded by any kind of clutter makes it almost impossible to create anything that might feel better to you. It just nags and nags, insisting you clean it up before you can go on to anything else.

So do it already. In 50 seconds, choose any one thing and get rid of it. Give or throw it away, or tag it for a rummage sale. Delete a bunch of old emails. Decline a meeting. Do it again and again, and eventually, the clutter that had you trapped will disappear.

Bye, bye density!

14
Give thanks

EVERY DAY, IN thousands of little ways, each one of us is blessed. There are sunrises and/or sunsets to admire. We are surrounded by kind people who work with us, serve us, lead us and love us, in spite of our failings or our unwillingness to acknowledge them in return. Of the trillions of chemical and other functions our bodies complete every day, most of them go so well that we are unaware of them. Most of us have food in our stomachs, a roof over our heads, access to medical and dental care and safe streets to walk on, which unfortunately, cannot be said for everyone in the world yet. But regardless of our life circumstances at the moment, we have free will, and minds that are totally under our own control if we want them to be.

If you thought about it, you could probably come up with tens of thousands of reasons to be thankful.

the problem at hand? Then look and see how others react to you: are they keeping their distance? Do a quick review of your internal organs--what hurts? Is your head throbbing? Is your neck tight? Is your heart racing? Take a good, hard look at what happens within and all around you when you are under stress. It's usually not a pretty picture.

What you see are clues to what you really want. Medical intuitives say that our bodies are speaking to us all the time in metaphors. For instance, if your neck hurts, who or what do you think is a pain in the neck? If your upper back is bowed, what is causing you to believe that you have the weight of the world on your shoulders? If your knee or your hip is painful, what makes you feel like you don't have a leg to stand on? Your body may be speaking to you with very clear messages. Listen.

Your life is talking to you, too. Your circumstances are a mirror of what you have thought and believed until now. What are they telling you? Have you been "dumped on"? Are you "broke" or "buried"? What would you have had to believe for these circumstances to be true?

How has all of this made you act? Do you rationalize being difficult? Do you forget to smile? Are you unwilling to help others?

Do a 50-second scan of yourself and your life. Take notes, either mentally or actually. Study them. When you feel you understand, forgive yourself. Make a mental promise that from now on, you'll look at yourself first before blaming, advising or withdrawing from others. Not only will you learn a great deal about what makes you happy or unhappy; you'll also discover that the fastest way to set yourself free is to fix yourself, rather than trying to fix others.

When you do, you'll likely notice something wonderful: the negative stuff stops showing up in your life as often. Over time, there's less and less reason to judge others or act in resistant ways. And when the negative does come up, you're likely to be more curious about it than upset.

Watch yourself. It's the best show in town.

3
Listen to your thoughts

WHEN YOU'RE NOT watching yourself, stop and listen instead.

One of the causes of energy density is when our thoughts fight our fears. Listen in, and you'll soon discover that the hubbub is usually much ado about nothing.

Sit down. Take out a pen and if you have one, an egg timer. For 50 seconds (ok—you can use a minute timer and give yourself 10 extra seconds), write down what you hear yourself thinking. Only one rule: No editing. Just the truth, please. Let it pour out of you, without any hesitation. Make a list of words, phrases or sentences that are rattling around your mind right now. What are you thinking about? Are you using words like *can't, isn't, don't, won't, not, never, ought, should.....?* Notice how hard you're being on yourself. You wouldn't be friends with anyone who talked that way to you, would you?

When your 50 seconds are up, look at your list. If it upsets or scares you, vow to yourself that you're going to start paying as much, if not more attention to the good stuff. Crumple up the list (if you wrote it on paper), and throw it away. Be done with it for now.

If you have another 50 seconds, try reframing your negative words, phrases or sentences to the way you'd like things to be. There may be a dream hidden in there, or the solution to a problem that's been plaguing you. Play with your negative thoughts until they come out sounding better to you. Ask yourself, what would improve this thought? and then write down your responses on a fresh sheet of paper. When you're done, throw away the first sheet, and refer to the second one throughout the day.

Feel better?

4
Tell your worries to shut up

IF YOU'RE IN no mood to listen to your worries, simply tell them to pipe down. Pretend they are a misbehaving child, and give them a direct order: "That's enough! No more of your whining and complaining. Quiet down." If the restlessness or stress persists, get firm: "I said, be quiet. Stop! I refuse to listen until you settle down."

Then do it. Imagine that your worries are on television, and you're holding the remote control. Press the mental Mute button. Although the images are still there, they seem almost silly without the words to make them come alive.

Alternately, you can imagine that you have a janitor in your brain. Imagine him or her sweeping up the mess and clutter of your thoughts and simply disposing of them.

As your stressful picture goes silent, so will your negative thoughts, at least for 50 seconds. When you're done, go do what you'd rather do—what feels better to you—instead.

P.S. If you want to, you can turn up the volume on your worries later. As for me, I change my mental channel, and let the sponsor—me—know that I'm not interested in watching that program again.

5
Listen to everybody else

YOU MAY NOT be as stressed as you think. Instead, you may simply be picking up on what you hear spoken or acted out around you.

Stop talking. Take 50 seconds to walk around your office or the local mall and start listening to what other people are saying and doing. What you hear and see will show you that most people, most of the time, are pouring all their attention into complaining about or fixing things that are wrong. They are bent over, barely breathing and stuck in their own mental mud.

Energy is contagious. Our etheric bodies (the energy field immediately adjacent to our physical bodies) can extend out 30 feet or more, and it contains the vibration of how we're feeling. So if you walk into a

meeting in a good mood but everyone there is dealing with a very intense problem, you are likely to feel
drained very quickly. Conversely, if you have had an
exhausting day but force yourself to attend a party
where everyone is having fun, you will probably get
your "second wind" and have a very good time.

Try these 50-second experiments: Jot a few kind
words and send them in an email, text, or on a piece
of paper and leave them on a colleague's desk. Share
one of the treats from your lunch with someone who
appears to be having a difficult day. Smile at someone
you see on the street. Tell your boss a joke. Chances
are good that they'll lighten up. Even if they don't,
you'll feel better, and discover that their problems
really don't have to be yours.

Listen closely, and you'll realize that maybe it's not
you at all. This enables you to turn up the volume of
what you want and how you want to feel. When you
do, other people's problems will likely fade into the
background of your life.

6
Stand/sit up straight

ANOTHER REASON WE feel bad is because we abuse our bodies. Junk food, alcohol, cigarettes and drugs aside, we are only aware of our posture after it has been hideous, because our body parts start screaming, "Get off me!" "Untie me!" or "I can't breathe!" Our necks are bent over our phones for hours each day. We hunch over when we work on our computers. We cross our legs at the knees, lean our elbows on the table and curl up in our chairs or on our sofas. Women wear shoes that destroy toes, turn calf muscles to stone and throw off spinal curvatures. Most of the time, we are completely mindless about how we are torturing our bodies. No wonder that eventually, they cry out in pain!

Sitting or standing cockeyed makes it more difficult for our veins and arteries to carry cleansing, life-giving oxygen to the muscles, nerves and tissues that need it. By sitting and standing up straight, we literally and metaphorically regain our balance.

Your mother was right: You look terrible all crunched up and hunched over. And you probably feel terrible, too. So if you want to feel better, elongate your spine, push back your shoulders, pull in your stomach, lift up your lungs and hold your head high. There's a reason winners look like that.

Next time, listen when your body's trying to tell you to straighten up. Take 50 seconds and do it, and unleash the energy that's been tangled up inside you.

7
Breathe

ONE OF THE reasons our thoughts aren't clear and our bodies ache is because they're starved. We normally breathe with only the top 20% of our lungs, which means that our brains could likely use more oxygen. "Oxygen bars," where people can go for a shot of O_2 rather than whiskey, are the newest way to boost sagging spirits.

If there's no such place in your town, you can still do it yourself. Put both feet flat on the floor. Sit up straight, but not stiffly. Rest your hands gently on your abdomen. Close your eyes, so you can tune out the negative things that may be happening around you.

Exhale completely. Imagine that you're cleaning out a lot of old, stale stuff. Then breathe in slowly and gently, starting from your abdomen. Let your belly start the breath—it will move outwards as you breathe in. Then lift the oxygen into the area behind your navel, then up from the bottom of your lungs to the top, into your throat and finally, landing somewhere behind your eyes. Hold it there for a few seconds if you can, and then release it slowly, going back down the way it came. Do it again. Start with three cycles; work your way up to ten or more. (Note: If you have difficulty breathing, see your physician.)

Even if you're not sitting at a desk or aren't in a situation where you can close your eyes, you can and should still breathe deeply. Try it the next time you're standing toe-to-toe with someone in a confrontation. Do it as you're walking along the street. Do it while you wait in line, or when you're caught in traffic and are running late.

Bathing your mind and body with oxygen is like taking an internal shower. You'll feel as though you've been washed clean of your stress.   And all it takes is 50 seconds.

But we're better at complaining than counting our blessings, because 1) our survival instinct keeps us constantly aware of what might pose a problem; 2) everyone around us mostly thinks negatively; 3) we practice thankfulness mostly on the Sabbath or major holidays, not daily; and 4) it's socially unacceptable to proclaim all that is going right in your life, as most people consider it boasting.

Whether you believe in a diety or not, saying thanks is a form of blessing, which creates a connection between you and what's yours to enjoy. If you're not keen on talking to God, try thanking other people for the blessings they bring to your life. Thank yourself when you "step out of the box" and do something wonderful for yourself that you wouldn't ordinarily do.

When we say thanks, we acknowledge the value we find in life. We add to others, and to ourselves. The religious among us stop cheating God and acting like spoiled children who are never satisfied with anything. The secular step up to the kinder, more appreciative aspects of themselves. Thanks flows energy from the heart into the here and now, which feels good to both the giver and the receiver.

Take 50 seconds and say thanks, and mean it. You'll love the way it feels.

15
Be *for* something

WE'D RATHER WORRY than work. We're better at complaining than championing. We are well aware of what we are against, but terribly unsure of what we are for.

So our energy gets stuck because at our core, we are designed to create. Resisting anything just keeps us stuck, mentally, physically and vibrationally. We know passionately and without a doubt that we want something to change, but we either think we don't know what to do or we're are afraid to start doing anything for fear of how things might turn out. But procrastinating or jeering from the sidelines doesn't make us feel better. In fact, it makes us feel much, much worse. The more we don't want to think about things we think are wrong, the more we do. There's a famous saying that is horrifically true: "You can't get enough of what you don't want." Pour your energy into trying to avoid a problem, and that problem is yours to keep. Guaranteed.

Instead of being against something, choose to be **_for_** something else. Instead of being against poverty, be **_for_** decent jobs or affordable housing. Instead of being against your teenage daughter's boyfriend, you can be **_for_** her intelligence and common sense. Instead of being against runaway personal spending, be **_for_** a sane, workable plan for both enjoying and investing your money.

Take 50 seconds and make a decision. Once you do, you'll know what to do to make the decision good, and you'll know when to start doing it. In 50 seconds, you can decide to help build a Habitat for Humanity House, or decide to make a donation. You can decide to get to know what she sees in her boyfriend, including some of his better qualities; or you can decide to have a commonsense conversation with her about their relationship. You can email your best friend and ask for the name of his/her financial planner.

Stop resisting and get focused. You'll feel a lot better if you do.

16
Say no

ONE OF THE greatest sources of energetic tension is our unwillingness to say no to anyone. Some of us are particularly practiced at this, and will do just about anything anyone expects of us, whether we want to or not. This is because we want other people to like and admire us, or because we don't want to risk conflict.

If you want to come through and do things for others: great. But if you don't, the fact that you never say no is going to deliver some new form of resistance and density to your life now. When you don't say no to what you don't want to do, it forces you to say no to something you'd rather do that would likely give you more energy. Are you losing family time; the half hour of exercise you were trying to fit in each morning; time to finish your own priorities at work; or volunteer commitments you love? Although your intellect might rationalize giving up these things, your spirit won't, and the conflict within will cause energetic distress that has a variety of unpleasant consequences.

Let other people offer you opportunities to join them in good work and causes, but stop allowing them to decide what, where, when or how you will be involved. Say no to anyone who tries to make you feel guilty. Say no to anything you don't truly believe in. Say no to just going along so you can get along. Say no to any job that makes you feel bad, sad or like you've been had.

This is true even for little things, like electronic communication. I recently heard someone say, "Email (and texts) is evidence of someone else's agenda." It's up to you to decide how and when it should fit into yours.

One important note: saying no to a task is not the same as saying no to a relationship. You can still value and embrace the people who want you to do something for them without taking on their burdens.

Take 50 seconds and decide where you want to say no. Then say it, kindly but firmly. It will clear the way for you to say yes to things that will flow more of your peace and purpose into the world.

17
Say yes

ONCE YOU HAVE learned to say no, you can find more peace and pleasure by saying yes to the people, things and experiences you want.

You know what these are. There are people you've always wanted to meet. Someone at work with whom you've been hoping to collaborate. Things you'd love to own, that you believe would bring you comfort and satisfaction for years to come. Experiences you've been too busy to consider, but feel old enough and wise enough to try.

Saying yes—opening our hearts as well as our time—is a new experience for most people. It scares many of us the first time we try it. "Are you nuts???" our negative voices start screaming the minute we consider something that would make us happy. "Spare yourself the disappointment! Forget it."

Tell your worry voice thanks for the advice, but you're going to say yes anyway. The instant you do, you will feel like someone took an ax and cut the shackles off your soul. You might hear a "Yahoo!" deep inside, or, for that matter, "Zippity Doo Dah!" Even if you're a little scared, you'll feel your energy ignite and make you tingle.

Saying yes doesn't mean that everything will turn out fine. That person you wanted to meet might not be as exciting or interesting as you hoped. The new china might have to be washed by hand. Going back to college or starting a new company is a lot of work. But none of that will matter, because by saying yes, you take control of your speeding brain poured its energy into an eager heart.

Take 50 seconds and choose what you want. Say yes. And start enjoying the energy of your new adventure.

18
Wait and see

SOMETIMES, WE AREN'T sure whether we want to say no or yes. The fastest way to shift your stuck energy is to simply wait and see.

There is a saying, "Either lead, follow, or get out of the way." When you wait and see, you are basically doing the latter. You stand aside mentally and physically, and let others run the show for a bit. Energetically, you're floating through time and space until you notice something that feels right and good to you.

Waiting isn't passive, however. Pay attention to what is happening around you. What you will see is creation at work. Whether it is constructive or destructive depends entirely on who is doing the leading and what his or her intention is. What is the goal of the current activity? Are things chaotic or organized? How does it feel to you? How do you think things will end, if they continue on the current path?

While you're waiting, stay tuned in to your own six senses, including your intuition. What messages or impulses are you getting? Do you want to move towards or away from where you are?

Normally, most of us are uncomfortable "doing nothing." But waiting is not doing nothing; it is a conscious act that can do something very powerful for yourself—it can help ensure that your next step is the right one for you. When things are changing and you're not the one making the changes, consider using it, even if for a mere 50 seconds. It could help save you new energetic road blocks later on.

19
Change the subject

THE BEAUTY OF life is that it is full of rich diversity. No two of us see things identically on every subject. The challenge of this, of course, is that sooner or later, you're going to encounter someone whose views and beliefs are very different than your own. Many people will then try to challenge and/or change these in the other person, either to prove themselves right or because they feel safer and more secure when everyone around them thinks as they do.

Fighting this battle is frequently exhausting, and often futile. So save the energy, and your sanity. Take 50 seconds and change the subject.

If the other person refuses or returns to the topic on which you cannot agree, say, "Let's agree to disagree on this topic," or I'd rather love you than fight with you." If they insist on hammering away, insisting that you are wrong, say, "my beliefs are right for me, and I'm keeping them for now." Then leave the room. Disengage from the idea that fighting is a pathway to peace. It's just energetic warfare that has no purpose other than to help some people feel more alive through anger and self-righteousness.

I have known many argumentative people in my life, and have been one myself. So I can say with certainty that the reason people do it is because they're scared. Scared that they might be wrong. Scared that their world might be out of control. Scared that you won't respect them if they're not right.

You can't do anything about their fears, but you can change the subject. One of my favorite ways to do this is to change the mood as well as the subject with a question like, "What good things have been going on in your life lately?" If they are stumped for an answer, try providing one yourself: "Your kids are absolutely adorable! I bet the younger one is just a whiz in school. What subjects does he enjoy?"

When life is over and we stand at the Pearly Gates, they say we are not asked what we accomplished, where we lived or how we atoned for our mistakes. Instead, supposedly all God wants to know is, "What did you learn about love?"

Love someone else. Love yourself. Change the subject.

20
Go a different way

ONCE WHEN WE were hiking with friends, we faced a 2000-foot mountain covered in sharp rocks at the higher elevations. There was a well-worn path up its face, but the trail obviously ended about half-way up, where the rocks began. "Let's walk around and go up the other side," our friend suggested. Although we had to rake our way through uncut territory, we made it. And the view from the top was breathtaking.

When it comes to challenges, most people begin by taking the well-trod path they and others have used before. When the path runs out, they stop before they reach their destination, either turning around and going back the way they came, but feeling dissatisfied and unhappy. They might try the path again, this time working "harder" or "smarter." But energetically, it's still the same, and they get thwarted every time. After a while, they come to believe that halfway up is as high as they can go not only on a mountain, but also in life.

The problem is that the "still, small voice" inside us refuses to be still at all because we know we want to get to the top to see what we can see from that vantage point. Our hearts keep whispering, "There's a way up. Go find it." We get a nagging feeling that we've failed somehow, which causes us to question our self-worth. And that further scrambles our energy.

So take 50 seconds and choose a new direction. Take your internal compass to guide you, and trust that you have more experience than you think in dealing with potential hazards of the road. If you encounter one, ask how you can go under, around or over it if you can't go through it, or how you might transform it altogether. Look in wonder at the new scenery at each stage. Rest along the way so you can savor how far you've come. And when you reach the top, realize that there is probably an even easier way for you to get back down again. This is true not only in hiking, but business, personal relationships and life-altering decisions of health, money and political views.

There is always another way. Find it, and you'll never be held back again.

21
Smile

IT TAKES FEWER muscles to smile than it does to frown, but that's not why smiling takes less energy than frowning. It's because when you do it, it's impossible to feel bad at the same time.

Try it and see for yourself. Go to a mirror. Put a great big happy smile on your face. Then tell yourself, "I feel rotten." You won't believe it, and you just might burst out laughing.

If you smile more, you'll be healthier, which is another reason to it. When you smile, you release chemicals in your body that enhance your immune system. In fact, if you smile a mere 15 times a day, you'll be 20% healthier than the rest of the American population. Being sick saps your energy. You'll feel better and brighter if you smile instead.

The other reason to smile is that when you aim one at another human being, they usually will smile back at you. It's almost impossible not to. It doesn't have to be a bare-your-teeth-and-grin-from-ear-to-ear smile. A soft, pleasant one will do just fine, thank you. Just think of something that makes you feel good, and you're off and running. You'll both radiate more.

So there you have it. In just a few seconds, you can feel better, and you can cause a chain reaction that makes everyone around you feel better, too.

Isn't that reason enough to smile?

22
Eat something soothing

YOUR GRANDMOTHER MADE it, and if your grandmother wasn't around, your mother probably did. Comfort food.

You know the stuff: Homemade chicken soup with skinny little egg noodles no longer than the top notch of your pinky, served to you in bed when you were sick. Rice pudding the consistency of melted marshmallows. Turkey with roasted chestnut dressing that you could smell in the attic as you were getting down the extra chairs for company. Anything warm and chocolate.

Food has always been a great comforter throughout the ages, because it both settles us down and fills us up. Every culture around the world has its own version of comfort food; it's whatever makes you feel satisfied and happy. After a good, satisfying meal, we're ready for anything, although usually, we don't crave anything. No matter how tense or dense our lives get, a homemade meal has a way of reminding us that the world isn't really falling apart and that every-thing's ok.

Comfort food doesn't have to be complicated. And you don't need an hour to eat it. Fifty seconds for just a few bites of a food you associate with fun or love will do the trick. Imagine a mouthful of a well-baked potato mashed with a fork and smothered in butter. A forkful of scrambled eggs and some cinnamon toast. And here's the magic: If it's impossible to obtain what you want because of where you are at the moment, just imagine it; your body will react the same as if you are actually eating it and you'll feel your energy return.

What matters is that the food-real or imagined- be homemade with loving hands (including your own) and savored slowly. And it should be warm. A big dish of ice cream smothered in chocolate sauce isn't comfort food. It's a treat, and one that isn't likely to leave you in the same state of mind—or belly--as a good plate of comfort food will. Comfort food not only feels good going down—it's always easy to digest.

So eat something soothing. Your restless soul—and your stressed-out body-- will thank you for it.

23
Hum

IT'S EASY, IT'S fun, and you can do it in under 50 seconds. Stop talking, close your mouth, and start humming your favorite tune.

If you don't have a favorite tune, then just hum whatever notes pop into your head. In Yiddish, this is called a *niggun*, a little melody that you make up in the moment.

The great thing about humming is that you don't have to stress out about remembering the words to the song. You don't necessarily even need to remember the melody. Just keep humming.

When you hum, you feel it in your head, but eventually, it spreads to your neck, throat and shoulders. Then down it goes into your arms and hands. It tickles your heart and makes your chest giggle. Sometimes you can feel it in your legs and feet. If that happens, it will make you want to dance.

Humming tunes us up and makes us smile. It brightens up your energy on the inside, which others can then see on the outside.

If humming tunes you up, don't be afraid to burst into song. You'll surprise everyone around you, but they just might throw in a harmony or two, and you'll all feel a lot brighter.

24
Send some love

WE'RE DESIGNED TO give and receive love. But when we're stressed, it feels like the flow of it stops cold.

So take 50 seconds and try thawing the ice. Send a sweet text to someone you love. Write a short email, with or without emoticons. Post a photo or a quote that stirs your heart on a social media site. Leave a kind or caring voice message for someone you know might not be available, but who would appreciate knowing you were thinking of him/her.

If you think you're not good at expressing yourself verbally or in pictures, simply sit and think, "I am choosing to send love to anyone who could benefit from it now." Just put it out into the universe. It's likely you'll be pleasantly surprised by what happens—you might hear from an old friend or meet a stranger who feels like family from the moment you're introduced. Alternately, you might find yourself feeling more com-passionate towards someone who has angered you in the past.

If you're angry at the world, send some love to your own heart. Turn your attention inward. Focus on the center of your chest, and just think or say, "I love you."

Dr. David Hawkins is the author of a book called *"Power Vs. Force."* In it, he has a Map of Consciousness, a chart of vibrational states and their corresponding emotions. On the chart, love logs a vibration of 500, which is just 100 small points away from peace and bliss. He also points out that the 500 level corresponds with the emotion of reverence. Imagine how differently you would feel and how much better things would likely go for you if you shifted from the reverses of stress to full-scale reverence.

If anger is what is locking up your energy, love is the key.

25
Affirm what you want

WE LIVE IN a noisy world. On the one hand, we're presented with millions of things we can own, do or become. On the other, there's so much variety that life can be pretty overwhelming at times. It's enough to tie your energy up in knots.

Decades ago, I learned that each of us (in the U.S.) was exposed to more than 250,000 advertising messages every day. This included everything from the label on our tubes of toothpaste to the dealer's insignia on the trunk of the car in front of us on the freeway. Today, thanks to hundreds of TV channels, the internet and more radio stations, newspapers and magazines than ever before, each of us is supposedly hit with more than two million messages a day. As a result, most of us don't know what we want. We know what we don't want, which are confusion and stress. But making one clear, solitary choice among the millions placed before us every day? Practically impossible.

But doing so will make all the difference in the world in terms of your stress level. And that's where affirmations come in handy. In less than 50 seconds, all you need to do is create one simple phrase that positively states what you believe what you would like to experience.

Start with what you think you need or want. For example: "I need a new car." However, know that the energy of need keeps you focused on the lack of what you want, which just creates more of it. So you'll need to focus on what would feel good or, at the very least, better. Try, "I enjoy owning a reliable car with less than 30,000 miles on it." You'll find that your attention suddenly narrows to quality used car ads or leases. Take, "I want a new job," and turn it into, "I like being the one in charge of a project." Exchange, "I'm too fat" with "I am getting in better shape every day." You'll undoubtedly attract equipment, classes and end-of-the-mall-parking spaces that begin making that vision come true.

Narrow the field. Affirm what you want at this time. Think incrementally. Winning the lottery or dancing on your desk if you're in the office isn't likely to work, but finding money in unexpected places or hearing music that makes you feel happy and free probably will. Get in the habit of believing that life will deliver through you, and for you. Because it will. When it does, celebrate the way energy works through you and for you.

26
Color

YOU LOVED IT as a kid, and now it's back. Coloring. The wonderful art of taking a black-and-white drawing and bringing it to life.

Years ago, you were lucky if you had a box of 8 crayons or maybe a few colored pencils. All you needed then was a pad of blank paper, or, for that matter, a few empty grocery bags. The black-and-white comics in the newspaper were fun to color, as were coloring books.

The wonderful thing about coloring when you were a kid was that there was no right or wrong way to do it. We were giving people blue hair long before anyone knew the term "heavy metal." We could grow grass on the clouds or make people live in trees and nobody cared. If we colored in a pre-printed book, we could press hard or soft, fill in the background or not. We could skip a page, work on the same one for days, or just color in the hair on every character. Coloring was a great way to express the possibilities of life without the worry of what the consequences might be.

Coloring is just as relaxing and fun today as it was then. Better, even, because now there are hundreds of coloring books in a myriad of subjects, fabulous markers that glitter and glow, and whole sets of crayons or pencils that have every hue of color imaginable.

If you're feeling tense, coloring for 50 seconds will shift your focus away from whatever is bothering you; it's a simple way to feel better, fast. If you don't have pencils or a coloring book at the moment, try doodling. Just grab the nearest writing instrument and let your hand roam free on any paper you have available. Coloring or doodling is not only relaxing; it can sometimes open up our inner genius and give you an "ah ha!" moment that is exactly what you need right now.

So when your life seems grim and gray, try coloring. It'll liven up your spirits, and possibly the face of your refrigerator, too!

27
Call a professional

THERE ARE TIMES when you feel as if you're in over your head, or you don't know where to begin, or you're in new territory. That's when it's time to call a professional.

There are professionals for every kind of problem. Financial experts can help you get out of debt or create a financial plan that will help you save money for your children's education or your retirement. Lawyers are not only for people in trouble, but are a great source of advice for those who want to start businesses, plan estates, buy real estate, protect an intellectual property or make sure their company can continue operating in the event of an accident or illness. Nutritional counseling can help you make sense of what you eat. A professional coach can help you in sports or at work. A professional carpenter can fix the mess you made in your do-it-yourself home improvement efforts. Psychological or psychiatric counseling can assist you in managing your anger, resolving relationship issues, finding your self-confidence, and much, much more.

There's a lot of good information available, and a lot of talented people to help you. To find the right person, take 50 seconds and ask a friend who they recommend; do a quick internet search to create a list of professionals in your area; or contact your Employee Assistance Program.

Working with a professional can make you feel a lot smarter and more in control of your life. It can also move you forward a lot farther, a lot faster. If you have another 50 seconds, make an appointment.

Hiring a professional is like handpicking the perfect guide to help you along a stretch of unmarked path on your life's journey. They can get take you over or around a block in your path, or help you chart a course so you never encounter a roadblock in the first place.

If you're the kind of person who thinks you need to do everything yourself, hiring a professional will remove the energetic burden of carrying the load yourself, and will align you with the outcome you really, truly want.

Grow for it!

28
Laugh

IF SMILING IS good for relieving stress, laughing is better.

Sometimes in our crazy, angry, seemingly out-of-control world, there doesn't seem to be much to laugh about. But take 50 seconds and look around. Ever see two dogs kissing? A baby playing peek-a-boo with an adult's hat? Two old friends sharing a joke on a park bench?

If the evidence of the fun in life still eludes you, check the internet videos for 50 seconds of fun, or go to a joke site and memorize a quick one.

In 50 seconds, you can make a date to go to a comedy club. Turn on the comedy channel in your car. Sign up for email delivery of jokes on a daily basis. Download a comedy album.

Laughter really is the best medicine. When you're laughing, you crowd out all your thoughts of stress and worry. And when that happens, all the chemical and other reactions designed to protect you from trouble back off temporarily. Your heart rate and blood pressure relax. Your muscles let go of their tension. Your head stops pounding. Your immune system is toned up. Literally and figuratively, you feel better.

While you're laughing at others, don't forget to laugh at yourself. Because in the end, one of the reasons you're stressed is because you're taking whatever is happening to you much too seriously. It may not be funny now, but ask yourself: "Will I laugh about this in five or ten years?"

Laugh. Lighten up. Fifty seconds later, you'll probably find yourself thinking, "What stress?"

29
Gather ideas

WHEN TENSION IS making you feel stuck, one of the fastest ways to get moving again is to start collecting life-improvement ideas.

There are many fun, easy ways to do this. Try "Life Shopping." Fifty seconds on Instagram or Facebook should do it. Or get a magazine or newspaper that features a lot of different kinds of people, especially the ones who are relaxed, happy and confident that they can make things happen. Read about them. See if you can learn more about their attitudes, interests and sources of support. Jot a few notes.

Then think of your friends, family members, celebrities—anyone you're aware of. Again, make notes about what you admire in their lives, and the qualities you've seen or heard them talk about that seem to contribute to their success.

If you know what you want, go online, send an email to a coworker or call your mother and ask: "How do I...?" "Where can I....?" "What do I need to do or learn to be able to...?" You'll be amazed at how many people are willing to help.

Take 50 seconds to start a Pinterest board. Or clip pictures from old magazines or other photo sources and start a scrapbook of things you love. Our minds think in motion pictures, so having a picture book is a great way to stimulate your imagination and direct your thinking more towards what you want. Look at the scrapbook often—twice daily or more, if you can. Fifty seconds is enough.

You can also get wonderful insights from 50 seconds of deep relaxation. Put your feet flat on the floor. Sit up straight. Watch your breath. Your intuition will flow freely, offering you new ideas to move you forward in ways that are right for you.

Shop around. And you'll soon have the blueprint for a happier life.

30
Go natural

THERE IS NO stress in nature. None at all. I have never met a tree that stands around worrying if it's doing the right thing, nor have I ever talked to a squirrel that apologized for gathering too many acorns.

Each living thing in nature offers something unique that compliments and harmonizes with the life around it. There is no competition; just an allowing that leaves us humans in awe. Nature doesn't think, doesn't compete, and doesn't try to be anything it's not. It just is.

So the next time you're feeling tense, get out in nature. What can you do in 50 seconds? Open a window and breathe some fresh air. If your office complex has an atrium or park, step outside for a minute, even in your imagination (remember: your body will think it's real.) If you can't leave your desk or you're in an urban area, keep a plant and gaze at it. Or find a nature video online and watch it for 50 seconds. Any of this will turn off the pressure and remind you that if you simply allow yourself to relax, you will find that you fit well in your environment.

While you're in this softer place, ask yourself how you are like the nature you're experiencing. Perhaps you are a willow tree, flexible and easily bent. Maybe you're a tall oak, reliable and firm. Are you the hummingbird that touches down for a moment of sweetness, or are you the gopher that knows how to burrow deep for protection? Look around, and you just may find the clues you're seeking to make your life better.

Remember to go beyond looking at nature to embracing it. Fifty seconds holding a well-worn rock can be very settling. Brushing a fallen feather against your cheek and savoring its softness feels like being touched by angel wings. Tuning in to a chorus of birds can transform even the most cluttered mind. Remind yourself that there are, indeed, many treasures in life that are free.

Nature knows this. Now you do, too.

31
Tell the truth

THERE ARE MANY reasons why many of us bend the truth, or don't speak it at all. Regardless, not doing so creates a lot of stress.

Even if you struggle with how you might want to tell the truth to someone else, it takes no time at all to admit the truth to yourself. Try it now, and you'll see. Find a mirror, or just use the reflection when your computer or phone screen is dark. Look yourself in the eye. Then tell yourself—out loud-- whatever you know you've been resisting or avoiding. Say it simply and honestly.

Often, it's a relief to do this. You may even start to laugh. Even if the truth is absolutely, positively something you know you want to avoid, cornering it in this way puts you back in control and allows you to start the process of deciding what you want to do next.

If you need to tell the truth to someone else, take 50 seconds to practice your approach, using the same reflective surfaces suggested above. Try to keep whatever you have to say as simple as possible. If you need help, get ideas from your favorite movie. "Houston, we have a problem." (*Apollo 13*)   "Toto, I don't think we're in Kansas any more." (*Wizard of Oz*) "Go ahead; make my day." (*Dirty Harry*)

While it may be hard to tell your parents you're gay, your boss that you're quitting, or your longtime lover that the feeling you once had is gone, telling the truth connects you to something vital in your spirit that unleashes the energy that makes miracles happen.

If you don't think you're lying to yourself or others, then consider this question, once posed by consultant Peter Block: "What is the 'yes!' you no longer mean?" In other words, where are you saying yes but wishing you could find the guts to say no?

Tell the truth and set yourself free.

32
Play "what if?"

WHEN WE GET stuck, we get stressed. When we say, "There's nothing I can do about it," or, "that's just the way things are," our voices go flat, our shoulders slump and our eyes stare at the floor, as though we're hoping it will swallow us up. It's no fun to feel shackled or cornered, and it destroys the flow of our energy.

If your life has stalled and you're not happy about it, take 50 seconds to play "What if?" You can play it alone, with another person, or with the universe. Start by asking the question, "What would I be doing now if I didn't believe I was stuck?" Grab the first answer that comes up from your gut, and mentally run with it.

Think about your answer, and then ask again: "What would I feel if I was doing this?" Get clear on the feeling, and repeat, "What difference would there be in my life if I felt like this?"

Pause once more, and allow your imagination to fill in some of the details. Mentally look at things like your relationships, your financial condition, your living quarters and your health. You will undoubtedly see that some or all of them improve when you feel like you're on a roll again.

Finish with, "What can I do right now if I want this pleasant change to begin?" Although you might not receive an instant answer from your subconscious, you will likely start noticing signals in your daily life that, if you follow them, will put you on the right path. Listen for hints in conversations. Watch the headlines in the newspaper. Walk into your local library or bookstore and see which books catch your eye. Meditate, day-dream or pray daily, opening up to your own inner voice.

What would the rest of today be like if you took the first step towards freedom and fun this very minute?

33
Take off your shoes

IN MOST OF our minds most of the time, there are places we need to go, people we need to see and things we need to do. We are always on the move, hurrying, scurrying, and rushing about. We run and run, not just after experiences and people, but also after time. We think it is running out, and that we must complete our "vital" missions first.

Several years ago, I took off my watch, and discovered that without it, I always seemed to have the time I needed to do whatever I wanted. Today there is no such luxury, as we are reminded of the time with every glance at our phones.

Instead, try taking off your shoes. When we are in our stocking or bare feet, we mentally relax, since it is a clear signal that we're not going anywhere for the moment. Taking off your shoes is synonymous with putting your feet up, whether you actually prop them on an ottoman or not. It represents a pause in the action, a break, a chance to feel the wind beneath your feet.

Literally and figuratively, taking off your shoes takes off some of life's pressure. We lace and stuff our feet into these little leather, vinyl, canvas and/or rubber vehicles, designed to move us, protect us, make us taller or decorate us. There is no doubt that they're wonderfully useful, which is all the more reason that shedding them, even for 50 seconds, feels so darn good. When we take them off, we don't have to be useful to anyone or anything. We can wiggle our toes and be ourselves. Before long, we're willing to put them back on and rejoin the game of life.

Take the pressure off. Take off your shoes. Your soul—and soles—will love you for it.

34
Delay the contact

THANKS TO TECHNOLOGY, there is almost nowhere on earth where you cannot be reached any more. Now, wherever we are, anytime of the day or night, people can communicate with us. It doesn't matter if we're in a stall in a public restroom, sitting in an opera house or walking down the street. There's no longer any place to hide.

That's the problem. Sometimes we don't want to be reached or interrupted. If we turn off the gadgets, our friends, family and colleagues say, "Why'd you do that? I was trying to reach you!" With all these forms of communication, it's easy to fall into the trap of using several of them simultaneously. You can listen to your voicemail at the same time you're receiving texts. You can talk on your cell phone while your email inbox is filling up and the caller ID on your desk phone insists that your boss is trying to reach you. Suddenly, everyone is talking to us at once, and it's tough to hear life, let alone the sound of your own beating heart, over the din.

All this contact adds up to a lot of additional pressure and stress, which just makes us tense and dense. There's just no excuse any more for not knowing or not responding. While cell phones have saved lives and voicemail has saved business deals, by and large, their convenience is balanced by the inconvenience of having more and more information we cannot ignore.

I'm not suggesting we go back in time or technology. But every now and then, you just might want to drop out for 50 seconds. Simply ignore all of your gadgets temporarily. All those people and all those tasks will still be waiting when you're done. But in the meantime, you'll be able to take a deep breath and come home to yourself.

It's a great way to get out of your head and back into your life.

35
Remember

YOU WEREN'T ALWAYS the person you are today. Even if you are young now, you were younger once. And likely, you felt much, much freer.

This is because kids keep things simple. Remember when a cardboard box made a great lemonade stand or fort? Remember when you didn't have nine players for your baseball team, so one person batted twice? Remember when licking ice cream cones in the shade on a hot summer day tasted better than dinner at the Ritz? Remember coasting downhill on your bike, feet out like wing flaps and the wind in your face?

You didn't think about where the money was going to come from then. You didn't much care what other people thought. You didn't worry about what might happen tomorrow or next month or next year, because today was all that mattered.

You were creative. You made do, and made things work. You paid your own way. You set yourself free.

And at the end of the day, you still went home, did your chores and your homework and went to bed at a decent hour.

If you didn't have an easy or a happy childhood, remember how you got through it and—hopefully—the day you realized that things were going to be all right for you. What got you to where you are today? Or watch the happy child of a friend or relative. What does s/he do that makes challenges simple?

That happy, strong or important person is still alive inside you. Remember how he or she did things, and apply that easy, unforced effort—or that tenacity, grit and dedication-- to whatever you're facing right now.

You don't have to be a kid again. Take 50 seconds to remember and you'll feel decades lighter.

36
Stare at a picture

EVERYONE I KNOW has lots and lots of pictures. This is because we always have a camera with us in our phones. Some have printed photos in albums, but mostly, our most memorable moments are captured in digital images that we share with our cyber-friends and family.

Unfortunately, few of us ever look at our pictures more than once. Once the images are replaced with new ones, we rarely, if ever, look at the old ones again. Even printed photos that get stashed in albums are often forgotten.

When it comes to relieving stress, that's a mistake. Because a happy picture can do more to lift our spirits and stir our creative imaginations that almost anything else. A photograph is more than a few happy faces with some background. It's your ticket to bringing to life everything about a moment, including the mood, the light in the room, what people were wearing, what was served and so much more. Sometimes, you can even hear music playing and people talking, if you listen with your heart.

Studying a happy picture for 50 seconds is easy and restorative. So the next time you're feeling stressed, find a photograph of people you love, a place you enjoyed or a moment that made you happy. Stop and study it. Notice every single little detail. Then close your eyes, and let the feeling of comfort pour through your body, washing you clean of tension.

Stare at a photograph, and you'll find that happiness is staring right back at you.

37
Focus on solutions

WE LOVE PROBLEMS. They give us something to do. If we had no problems, life would be very boring. Toss a problem in the mix, and things start to get exciting.

But there is a problem with problems. They make us feel bad, and mess with our energy. They cause us worry and tension. They make us snap at our children and afraid of our boss. They cause us to wonder if we're strong enough or smart enough to overcome them. So while we're dealing with them, we don't sleep, eat or love very well. And if they're particularly big, they overshadow the good in our lives.

The way most people deal with problems is a problem, too. They keep looking at what's wrong, what made it wrong in the first place, and what's likely to go wrong because of it in the future. Their entire focus and concentration is on what's wrong, wrong, wrong. Unfortunately, the more they do that, the bigger the problem gets, both in their minds and in reality, because anything you pay attention to expands. And it isn't long before a problem becomes a crisis.

So the next time you're faced with a problem, take 50 seconds and think about what a solution might look like instead. A solution is not something you do in response to trouble, but rather, something you do to replace it entirely. Look at what's wrong and say, "What do I/we want _instead_ of this?" Then, rather than trying to repair a broken piece of life, you can have the fun and challenge of creating something newer and better to replace it. Why patch when you can weave? Why make do when you can make over?

Problems are opportunities in disguise. They're daring you to be bigger and bolder and better than you were before. They're life's way of saying, "Create, oh wonderful one!"

Replace your problems with solutions. And watch your energy return.

38
Snap your fingers

IT'S AS EASY as one, two, three. The next time you're feeling really tense, close your eyes, put your thumb to your middle finger, and SNAP!

The purpose of doing this is to literally snap you out of it. If you've really worked up an emotional lather, you may have to snap the fingers of both hands at once to wake you up. Or you can go back and forth, snapping one hand and then the other, until you are restored to a more harmonious rhythm with life.

The wonderful thing about snapping your fingers is that you don't need any special equipment to do it. Your hands go where you do, so you're all set. Some people put big thick rubber bands around their wrists and snap them when their thoughts get out of hand, but personally, that idea doesn't appeal to me very much because it looks terrible and it hurts.

Snapping your fingers is much easier and a lot more fun. If you really want to jazz things up, think of a song you can hum while you're doing it.

Snapping your fingers has the effect of a hypnotist at the end of his act. He'll say, "When I snap my fingers, you'll come out of your trance, and you won't remember anything that's happened to you." From time to time, all of us could use that, especially when our runaway stress makes our words or our behavior get out of hand. And it only takes a second to do it.

Unlock your power. SNAP!

39
Get sense-able

MOST OF US have five treasures we take for granted. Our senses. Without them, life would be flat and uninteresting. With them, we are rich.

Which is why so many people feel poor. We rarely savor the incoming messages brought to us by our five senses. If we notice anything at all, it is only in passing, as we move on to the next moment and the next. As a result of using our senses so poorly not only do we fail to get deep and lasting satisfaction from our experiences, we hardly get any satisfaction at all.

On my wedding day, a friend gave me some wonderful advice. "Pay attention to what your senses pick up," she said. Decades later, I can still smell the roses I carried, hear the whispers of my friends and family as I walked down the aisle, taste the faint waxy flavor of my lipstick, feel the crispness of the silk organza of my dress and see Steve smiling as he waited for me at the pulpit. Having that one sensory experience not only made my wedding day wonderful, but it has served me well since then, especially when marital challenges have come.

Although you naturally use all five physical senses at once (assuming all five are functioning), take 50 seconds and focus on them for 10 seconds at a time if you hope to enrich your experience. Use your sight to zoom in on a small detail of something close to you. Then close your eyes and listen. Don't just hear: Listen closely for ten seconds. You will be amazed at all the sounds there are in the world, and how many of them are layered in any given moment.

With your eyes still closed, take in a deep breath through your nose—five seconds in; five out. Pay attention not only to what you smell, but how it makes you feel. Smells have great power over us, and can conjure up memories. If you're not actually eating something, ask yourself: What is the flavor of this aroma? Give yourself 10 seconds to decide. Finally, touch something, or get a feeling in your heart before you open your eyes.

Get sense-able, and let this moment reenergize you.

40
Turn it off

YOUR MOTHER WAS right: you do watch too much TV. It was bad enough when there were just a handful of channels. But now there are hundreds of channels. And unfortunately, more things to agitate and upset us than ever before. The news is mostly negative. Reality TV shows humanity at its worst. Movies are more violent than ever. Even most sports contests have an edgy, agitating feel to them these days.

Consuming these shows lowers your vibration to the level of what you're seeing on the screen, especially if you relate to it strongly. The lower your vibration, the worse you'll feel, as emotions like shame, anger, fear and desire are some of the biggest energy killers around.

If you're a constant TV watcher, remember the saying, "Neurons that fire together, wire together." By frequently stimulating your brain with violence and negativity, you're going to create repeated thought about what you don't want, which eventually will get hard-wired into your brain and you'll start expecting to see terrible things in the world around you, not just on the small screen.

The remedy is simple: take the remote and turn it off, or take 50 seconds to find a program that uplifts you.

When you do so, you just might find that you turn on something much better, like a show that's funny or uplifting; the sound of a loved one's voice; or echoes of peace within you.

41
Admit it

AN AWFUL LOT of people divorce their spouses or their jobs because they say they aren't getting enough satisfaction from them. When that happens, the bewildered partner or boss says, "I had no idea you were so unhappy!"

It's very, very hard to admit there is something we want. But there's no way around it. We were born to create, so once a desire arises in us, there's no going back. There's something we want to do or be or have or experience, and once we know what that is, we obsess over it until it's ours. The obsession isn't the same for everyone, particularly in its expression. But the thought and the yearning is always there, nagging, demanding we pay attention to it, either in our waking moments, or in our dreams.

In the movie, *"The Horse Whisperer,"* Robert Redford's character says, "The hard part is not having the thought. It's saying it out loud." That's true. Like being honest, the hard part is saying it out loud, first to ourselves, and then to others. We're afraid that they might call us selfish, unrealistic, crazy or just plain wrong. We worry that they'll somehow crush our dreams and spoil our good intentions. Or we worry that we're not up to the challenge.

Fantasies are wonderful escapes from reality. So are rationalizations. But ultimately, admitting what is in your heart is the only true relief. Even if what you admit you want never comes true, you've found the courage to say that you believe your life can and should be better. You've not only broken through a big, big barrier of resistance; you've also established a powerful connection to something that is life-affirming and energizing for you.

Start small. Take 50 seconds and write it down. When you're ready, take another 50 seconds and read it out loud several times. Then move on to someone you trust, or perhaps a total stranger who will not judge you in any way. You might be surprised by the kindred spirits you find, the supporters, or perhaps even the fans.

Admit that you're ready for more life, and life will rush forward to help you have it.

42
Stop contradicting yourself

I ONCE HAD a coaching client who had the quirky habit of shaking her head no as she was saying yes. When I pointed this out to her, she didn't believe me, so I took the compact out of my purse, held up the mirror and showed her. "Am I really doing THAT?" she asked with comically raised eyebrows. We both laughed.

Many of us contradict ourselves in countless ways. We say we don't have time for something as we're doing that very thing. We say we dislike a particular food, and then eat it anyway at a dinner party because we don't want to upset the host. We say we hate certain parts of our jobs, but comply rather than suggest alternative approaches. We have a strong intuition not to do something, but then do it anyway.

When we contradict ourselves, we create energetic tension internally that not only impacts our moods in negative ways; it also is broadcast into our environment, producing more of what we likely don't want.

So if things aren't going smoothly for you, take 50 seconds to look for contradictions between what you're saying and doing or between what you're thinking and feeling. You'll likely see where you are constructing barriers or attracting problems for yourself.

As your mother likely used to say: Stop doing that.

43
Chat

WHEN BABIES LEARN how to talk, everyone gets excited. Finally, they can respond to us, and we know what's on their minds.

But it isn't long before we start saying, "You're making too much noise. Pipe down!" This advances to, "Stop arguing with me!" Eventually, usually when they're teenagers, we find ourselves saying, "Shut up, will you?"

By the time we're adults, we know how to complain, yell, argue, mumble and whisper. We use words like weapons. But we don't have a lot of practice in just good old chatting. Chatting is a wonderful stress reliever, and a lovely way to talk to someone without putting a lot of pressure on either one of you. Conversations don't always have to have a point. It can be very relaxing to just chat.

Chatting revolves around a topic neither one of you cares very much about. It's a simple game, one that is very easy to play. The first person offers a non-offensive comment about something that is happening in that moment. The other person adds an insight or two of her own, and lobs the verbal ball back.

The beautiful thing about chatting is that you can do it anywhere, any time. In the checkout line at the grocery store. In a members only room on a website. With your kids, in a few texts. More often than not, it lasts less than 50 seconds. If no one is around right now, think back to the last chat you had with someone. Since the human mind does not know the difference between a thought and an actual experience, you'll still benefit.

Occasionally, chats turn into real conversations. But mostly, they don't. Two or more people just exchange a few pleasantries, and that's that. There's no real point. You do it because you can, not because you have to.

So chat. It's fun, it's friendly, it feels good, and it keeps your energy flowing.

44
Eat right

WE ARE TERRIBLE to our bodies. We starve them of sleep, and feed them all kinds of trash we know isn't good for them.

None of us would willingly dig in a garbage can for our dinners, but are perfectly willing to pour nutritional junk into our guts daily. I know people who live on coffee and ice cream bars. I've seen others put nothing but soda pop and bags of snacks into their grocery carts. I've listened to people brag about how they haven't eaten a vegetable in 30 years.

Then they wonder why they get sick. Feeding your body is not a lot different than putting gas in your car. If you give it less than it needs, it won't run very long before it conks out. If you put in poor quality stuff, it will sputter and perform badly. If you overstuff it, you run the risk of explosion. Put sugar in a gas tank, and your car won't run at all. Your body doesn't react a lot differently to it.

Even those who try to eat well sometimes eat wrong because they eat too fast. Americans are the world's fastest eaters, and it doesn't benefit us. We eat while we're driving, standing up, walking down the street or leaning on a countertop as we're out shopping. Most of the time, we're done in 15 minutes or less. We love fast food, fast lunches, fast cooking. But when it comes to digestion, our bodies want us to slow down. People in the rest of the world know this.

No one needs to be told how to eat right. The information is everywhere. All we have to do is come to the realization that you are what you eat, and start making choices of how you want to feel.

Take 50 seconds and choose a nutritionally vibrant food. The greener or more colorful it is, the better (and no, colored candy doesn't count). It doesn't matter if you eat it now or later. If your diet is already pretty good, take 50 seconds and chew your food more slowly so you can get more flavor, nutrition and satisfaction from it. If you really don't know where to start, take 50 seconds and do an internet search for nutritionists who live in your area, or online services that can help you.

Eating right doesn't mean that you can never have your naughty foods again. You'll just feel a lot less guilty, and be able to undo the damage they cause a lot faster.

Eat right, and get more energy from everything you eat.

45
Finish something

NO MATTER WHAT we are doing, we are never done. When we wash the dishes, our minds drift to the pile of laundry in the basement. When we're riding in a train, we're thinking about how we'll find a cab when we get to our destination. When we're having a conversation, we're concentrating on what we're going to say next, not on what the other person is saying at the moment. We're always thinking of the next thing, not the thing that is happening in that moment.

This is one of the reasons that many people will answer the question, "What did you do all day?" with a single word: "Nothing." This is because they were so busy thinking about what they didn't get done, they didn't enjoy any of what they did.

There is great anxiety in this that messes with our energy, because no matter how many tasks we perform or chores we do, we will never, ever get things utterly and completely "done." As long as we're alive, there will always be something we have to or want to do. Desire only stops when we die.

But all it takes is 50 seconds to change this. Finish whatever you're doing in this moment. Reading a paragraph. Writing a short email. Listening to a comment. Adding a line to a spreadsheet. Walking down the hall to get a cup of coffee. Wherever you are, whatever you're doing, pay attention to that one thing, and only that one thing. Finish it. Then do the next thing, and the next, and the next.

Not only will you lose the terrible fear that you're falling behind; you'll also gain enormous satisfaction from the activities you do. And from this place of personal peace, your future arises, which is bound to be more fulfilling.

Assuming you are awake approximately 16 hours a day, you have 1152 chances to take 50 seconds and finish whatever you're doing.

Why not start now?

46
Stretch

STOP RIGHT NOW. Put this down. Clasp your hands together, point your fingers to the ceiling, and raise your arms over your head like a steeple. Breathe.

Doesn't that feel better? We live in cubicles, cars and cramped positions that shorten our muscles, trap our nerves and compress our organs. As a result, we ache. We also take in less oxygen than we should, which makes us tired and confused.

The remedy is simple. Stretch. Get a good book, go to a class at a health club or ask your doctor. Learn how to properly and completely stretch the muscles in your body, so that they can be flexible and free.

Stretch any time you've been inactive for a while. Stretch when you first get out of bed in the morning. Stretch after you've spent an hour at your desk. Get out of the car and stretch after you've been on the road awhile. Stretch after you've just spent hours reading or watching TV. Stretch before you get into bed.

Stretch whenever you find your opinions getting rigid or your fatigue rising. Feeling stiff and sore is not just a medical condition—it's a metaphor for a state of mind that suggests you might need to be more flexible. Start by flexing your body, and see if new ideas don't enter as well.

Stretching is a way to keep yourself alert and energized throughout a long day. It wakes you up and takes the pressure off, literally and figuratively. And it takes less than 50 seconds to do it.

Feeling stuck? Stretch.

47
Offer praise

THERE IS A terrible shortage in our world, one that threatens to starve every man, woman and child on the planet. We are running out of praise.

By the time most of us are adults, we have forgotten what a kind word sounds or feels like. We are shaped by what we are told we cannot do and what isn't right. We are told that praise will give us a "swelled head," whatever that means. Meanwhile, we get smaller and more unsure of ourselves, finding it harder and harder to reach our full potential.

The situation only gets worse as time goes on. Job reviews are usually based on what needs to be improved in our performance, not on what we are doing right. Spouses will quickly point out what we haven't done, but tend to overlook what we have. Friends may offer a compliment or two, but even then, there's little more to say than a quick "Thank you." Praise is a scarce commodity. As a result, we eventually grow to feel as though we aren't enough, don't have enough and that nothing we ever do will be enough. A lack of praise is like a hole in our hearts. We can live with the condition, but it limits us.

The place to start a "Praise Parade" is in your own heart. The next time something works out, tell yourself, "You did that right!" If you wake up in the morning, try thinking, "Good going! You're still alive!" Raise your expectations of yourself slowly and surely. "You're always dependable." "Your laugh makes everyone smile." "You can do it!"

Once you have refilled your own spiritual well this way, you're ready to start offering to sincere and meaningful praise to others. Look for the good in them, just as you did with yourself. When you find it—and you will—offer a sentence of praise. Keep it short and simple, enough to encourage but not embarrass them. It takes less than 50 seconds, and it makes both of you feel great.

Feed your soul. Feed the world. Praise.

48
Slow down

THE PACE OF our lives is fast, and getting faster all the time. We go so fast both mentally and physically that we can't see what's headed our way until WHAM! There's an accident. We send off an angry email without slowing down to consider how it might be received. We rush through meals, and then feel bloated and sick afterwards. We fill our days with back-to-back meetings, forcing us to rush from place to place or call to call.

All too often, there's a big, ugly mess to clean up, energetically and actually. And even if there isn't, we just don't feel very good about ourselves or our lives.

There's a reason there are yellow caution signs at blind curves in the road. If you don't slow down, there's a chance you could lose control or collide with something you can't see. I'm talking about more than cars. Think about your past week. What person or problem did you "run into"? Did you crash and burn on a project? Did you get sideswiped just as you thought you had rounded a dangerous turn in your own life? How much emotional damage did you suffer? How much of it could have been prevented if you had taken things a little more slowly and thoughtfully?

Going slow is especially important when we are under stress. Take something that you normally do and slow it down. If you think something should take 25 seconds, try 50 instead.

Slow down. Keep your eye on the road before you and up ahead. If you'll do, you'll probably get to where you want to go much faster, because you won't need detours for the trouble you didn't cause.

49
Get ready

MANY OF US not only end our days stressed, we start them that way, too. From the moment we open our eyes, we start thinking about what we have to do, where we have to be and how we're ever going to get it all done. By the time we've brushed our teeth and combed our hair, we're a restless wreck.

This is the true definition of "getting out of the wrong side of bed." There's nothing wrong with our mattress; it's our thinking that's pushed up against the wall.

So tomorrow, start your day off right. Turn off the alarm. Roll over and put a smile on your face. Lie there, still, warm and content, and tell yourself just one thing: "I am ready for happiness." It all takes less than 50 seconds to do.

Get ready for happiness each and every morning. Look for it not just in what life brings to you, but in what you bring to life. Each day, add a little more of the good in you to the world. Giving happiness away to others is the fastest way of acknowledging that you are amply supplied.

If you don't want to wait until tomorrow, do it right now. Begin your day again in this moment. Simply think, and then say, "I am ready for happiness." Smile. Then go out and either give it, or allow yourself to receive and appreciate it.

You can get ready for happiness many, many times in a busy day. Put your thoughts straight, gather your feelings and make them presentable, and then go forward.

Get ready. If you keep this up, your life is going to get much, much happier.

50
Trust

THE MORE YOU come to practice and realize that life neither has to be overly stressful or difficult, the more you will be able to trust in the energy flow of life itself.

If you need evidence of how it works, go back to nature. You'll see that life sustains and balances itself quite nicely without interference. Even a raging forest fire produces ash that feeds new growth.

The earth has held this orbit for eons. The tide of every ocean is alternately high and low. If you go high enough on any mountain, you will find snow. No matter what is happening now, the weather will change eventually.

The same rhythms and balances are true for us. For all the evil, there is also great good. (If you're not seeing it, look again.) For every heart torn by tragedy, there is great love waiting to help it heal. For every soul at war, there is another equally impassioned for peace. For every global problem, there are people committed to fixing it.

The one thing you can count on is that life goes on. Somehow, some way, even with all the changes you've been through, you are still here. Amazing, isn't it?

Take 50 seconds and come to trust that there's something larger than you making life work. Even if today's a mess, tomorrow is bound to be better. And if not tomorrow, then next week, next month or next year. It's the way things work.

Relax and feel the flow. Trust. Remember that everything works out all right in the end, and if it's not all right, it's not the end.

About the Author

Robin L. Silverman believes in happiness and the creative power of the human spirit. She is the inventor of Fullistic® Living.

For more information on her classes, retreats and services, see her website: www.fullistic.com

Made in the USA
Monee, IL
29 April 2022